Wisdom Writers around the World

Aphorisms *Explained*

John W. Lorton

Inspiring Voices®
A Service of Guideposts

ISBN: 978-1-4624-0302-8 (e)
ISBN: 978-1-4624-0301-1 (sc)

Inspiring Voices books may be ordered through booksellers or by contacting:

Inspiring Voices
1663 Liberty Drive
Bloomington, IN 47403
www.inspiringvoices.com
1-(866) 697-5313

Printed in the United States of America

Inspiring Voices rev. date: 09/13/2012

Dedication

People everywhere love to quote words of wisdom from the greats of the past and from present writers and speakers.
This book is dedicated to those who seek a contemporary depth of meaning and explanation of some of the greatest quotations ever given.
And to Eveleen Lorton whose constant questioning encourages explanations beyond surface thought.

Contents

Aphorisms From The Famous And Not So Famous

Aphoristic Children's Stories: Aesop's Fables

Introduction

What Is An Aphorism?

A N APHORISM is a short and concise positive statement that expresses a wise principle or truth. It is not political or humorous but it does border on the philosophical. With aphorisms one is forced to use one's mind in a new way. The more you think about a particular aphorism the richer in meaning it becomes. An aphorism is frequently described as a "terse statement of a fact or a truth," and aphorisms have even been humorously referred to as answers to questions no one has asked.

1

Because aphorisms seem impossible to define they are variously described; for example, a Ukrainian writer says an aphorism is a "one line novel." However, the English poet and critic, Samuel Coleridge (1772-1834) wrote:

> **The largest and worthiest portion of our knowledge consists of aphorisms.**

Aphorisms have been with us from ancient times to the modern era, only they were not always called aphorisms.

Influence Of Wisdom Writers

There is nothing new under the sun. What is now new in our remarkable technological advances may only be the revealing of ancient knowledge that has been lost and is re-merging again and again. Great nations have risen and fallen and others have completely vanished. Even magnificent structures have been built and lost forever due to the ravages of time, water, and sand — even armies.

So it is with truths and insights that were written centuries ago...many lost and some found. These early writers have been referred to as *wisdom writers*.

Due to the many natural phenomenal events and even human prejudices, mountains of knowledge have disappeared. Could it be that ancient legends and myths were not really myths at all? Or have we just lost track of their world. It could be the same with ancient ideas and expressions that we are now rediscovering. Consider, for example, what an ancient Kung Fu master taught:

> When you look for the truth outside
> yourself, it gets farther away.

What another wisdom writer, Sun-Tzu (722?-481 BCE) wrote could apply to our 21st century problems:

> If you know the enemy and know yourself
> you need not fear a hundred battles.

Without a doubt the early writers, who we now call *wisdom writers* are relevant today. An ancient proverb has stated clearly what was true then is appropriate today:

> Managers do a thing right;
> leaders do a right thing.

Some of the early writers dealt not only with war or even with what we now call philosophy but with their gods and their personal passions and ambitions. Some of those ancient writings were quite perplexing or even baffling but they were always thought-provoking. In this regard some of the early writings were riddles and proverbs.

> "Many of the wisdom writers were fathers or
> teachers and their sons or disciples were to
> copy and memorize their lessons so as to
> serve as guides in later life. These wise men
> were considered to possess knowledge about
> how to live skillfully. Much of this wisdom
> is recorded in the Book of Proverbs in the
> Bible. Of wise men Solomon was considered

the greatest. He wrote and spoke three
thousand proverbs and his songs numbered
a thousand and five…" (Wikipedia)

Much of the ancient writing was not so much to teach facts and information as it was to challenge existing thought. It is from these early wisdom writers that aphorisms were born.

Influence Of Fortune Cookies

(A temple in Japan has a tradition of random fortunes, called omikus.)

According to Jeffrey Lee (2008), the fortune cookie was "introduced by the Japanese, popularized by the Chinese, but ultimately consumed by the Americans." The fortune cookie, however, did not stay popular very long in China because it was "too American."

That crisp little cookie made from flour, sugar, vanilla, and oil with a piece of paper inside, usually contains a fortune following the Japanese temple tradition of random fortunes.. Actually, the origin of the fortune cookie is probably unknown.

In the United States the cookie caught on rather quickly primarily because of that piece of paper inside. Those fascinating little slips of paper originally contained words of faux wisdom, or a vague prophesy, or even a list of lucky numbers. But it was not long in America, however, that those pretty little slips of paper were containing the actual

Chinese proverbs with translations as sayings and legends from some of the older wisdom writers, such as;

Honor your errors as hidden intentions.

Be a lamp unto yourself.

The fortune cookie's use of maxims and aphorisms from the Classical Period was a popular "fortune" at one time and many people started taking them seriously. It was Schiller (1755-1805), the German poet and philosopher, who warned people to listen carefully to those who speak much and say little, when a fortune cookie quoted him:

**Do not think the lion was sleeping
simply because he did not roar.**

Even the famous maxim from Thomas Jefferson (1743-1826), appeared in a fortune cookie, warning us to be careful of big government:

**Government big enough to supply everything
you need is big enough to take everything
you have. The course of history shows that
as government grows, liberty decreases.**

America's appetite for philosophical thinking did not last long and the fortune cookie soon became the source for light satirical advice, as in,

Go to college or starve.

Don't be humble. You are not that great.

Soon you will come into a lot of money.

Today all fortune cookies do not contain prophesy much less a classical maxim or an aphorism, but tradition holds that if you desire your fortune to come true you must eat the entire cookie.

Aphorisms

As mentioned previously, aphorisms cannot be defined but they can be described and they can be compared to other sayings such as quotations, adages, maxims, or proverbs. The difference between most sayings and aphorisms is that aphorisms are usually short pointed statements full of meaning and substance and they are factual and truthful, even when they are taken out of context.

Many *quotations* and *sayings* tend to be humorous or feel-good verse, that Hallmark is famous for, or other light statements and sentiments that are easily understood, usually agreeable, and pleasant to read. They are usually the kind of statement that makes you want to say, "O. Yes, I agree with that."

Not so with aphorisms. The aphorism knocks you off your feet because you do not quite understand or, at first glance, you may not agree. It is like a favorite tune – it stays with you because you cannot get it off your mind.

An aphorism in not merely an old statement accepted as a truth because it has been around for a long time. That is an *adage*, like, *"The early bird gets the worm."* We have heard that adage since childhood. Another recently revived adage is Finegal's Law – *"Anything that can go wrong, will."*

As compared to an adage, a *maxim* is a statement that is rather specific and factual and based on actual experience. Maxims are usually profound statements about our way of life:

A man ought never to let himself become a burden upon anyone.

Or as Henry Felding has said:

> **Look, Mr. Billifel, it has been my**
> **constant maxim in life to make the**
> **best of all matters which happen.**

Probably the most well-known maxim of all is Benjamin Franklin's:

> **He who hesitates is lost.**

A maxim is a statement that is reasonable and prompts a response of, "Yes, that is good and I think I understand it. And it is worthy of trying to live by."

When the American logician-philosopher, Charles Pierce (1839-1914), wrote the maxim, *"Let us not pretend to doubt in philosophy what we do not doubt in our hearts,"* he was close to Descartes's maxim, *"We should begin by doubting everything",* and from his own maxim Descartes aphorized:

> **I think, therefore, I am.**

Aphorisms are not to be confused with ***proverbs***. Most proverbs are usually easy to remember, particularly those that are poetic or alliterative, and are not usually difficult to understand, as in the 1735 edition of *Poor Richard's Almanac* when Benjamin Franklin coined, *"Early to bed and early to rise makes a man healthy and wise."* To this, Carl Sandburg suggested that if you follow Franklin's advice you will never meet any prominent people. Franklin's proverbs, however, are interesting to read:

Well done is better than well said.

A lie stands on one leg, the truth on two.

To err is human; to repent divine."

Franklin's proverbs may be clever and they do give us interesting descriptions of aspects of American culture, but they are not aphorisms.

Aphorisms do not entertain and they are not concerned with whether you like them or not. They are very brief statements of fact and that's it. An example of this is Montaigne's (1533-1592), aphorism:

Sits he ever so high on throne, a man still sits on his bottom.

Many minimalist decorators live by Robert Browning's (1812-1889) famous aphorism:

Less is more.

One of my favorite aphorisms is by Jackie Mabley (1889-1975):

> **If you always do what you always do, you will always get what you always got.**

Whether you like aphorisms or not they are always clear and to the point, and sometimes harsh or even sarcastic, as illustrated by the following two aphorisms by Ambrose Bierce (1842-1913):

> **A person of low taste is more interested in themselves than in me.**

> **The covers of this book are too far apart.**

It has been said that aphorisms are like the front teeth in humans, they cut through the food to make it more palatable.

Even though an aphorism is said to be the final word, it sometimes does need an explanation to put it in perspective and in everyday language what the aphorist is saying. *That is the purpose of this book – to present some philosophical gems and then offer a brief explanation of what the aphorist is saying – or even why it was said.*

JWL

Unwrapping Selected Aphorisms

The End Justifies
The Means.

Micolo Machiavelli (1469-1572)

I REMEMBER FROM my college days that **the end justifies the means** meant that winning is everything. I even remember that this was said by Machiavelli in his book, *The Prince,* in which the prince was advised to follow the political principles and methods of craftiness and cunning, even dealings that were deceitful and double-dealing. To me that seemed to say that in those days the goal was to control and maintain power no matter how you did it – just win.

Those college days are long gone but I am still having trouble applying this aphorism, **the end justifies the means**, to my 21st century life. I have lived through many wars from WWII onward with the noble goal of preserving peace, liberty, and democracy, but one cannot help but notice that the means used to reach that noble goal were truly and terribly severe. In my college textbook that was called "negative consequences" – that is if the act is negative, the consequence (the end) is negative.

Consider this: we all know that lying is wrong but are there times when lying is acceptable, even though it may be wrong, and even though some good may come from lying? Should lying be used to obtain a good end? To this end, ethicists might say that even though lying (means) was not right and even though the outcome was good, it tells us more about the person's character than the event itself; a person is not above lying to prove a point. Is this saying that anything is acceptable if it leads to a good result? Or, as my college prof put it, "Is it all right to sin because everybody does it?" Others might say, however, that the nature of the act is wrong regardless of the ends accomplished.

This idea can be carried to extremes. Hitler tried to prove his ideas of racial supremacy with completely unacceptable means. And the histories of some religions tell of horrific means some have used to glorify their gods and to spread their religious ends. It is as if a desired outcome excuses any good or bad means to attain it.

Examples are everywhere: politicians make outrageous promises and use illegal funds toward the end of winning the election. Or a romantic relationship may promise the moon to achieve a desired goal or end.

If we believe that **the end justifies the means** then it follows that we believe anything is acceptable if it leads to a desired successful result, and use of deceptive and other questionable means are justified.

All of this has existed since ancient times and may be the generally accepted method of thinking – the *modus operandi* – in today's world. But that does not make it good nor necessarily bad.

Another way of looking at this rather than through Machiavellian eyes is this: We are more apt to achieve morally positive and helpful ends if we use morally right means and actions. It may not always work that way because even morally right action may result in unfortunate ends, but in an effort "to do no harm" it seems to me that morally right actions have a better chance of producing morally right results than otherwise, In this way, ***the end justifies the means.***

I Think, Therefore, I Am.

Rene Descartes (1546-1650)

ANYONE WHO has ever wondered if they exist or not has the answer embedded in the question. The very fact that you wonder is proof of the fact that you exist. Otherwise you could not wonder.

To me that is very logical and easy to understand because existence is presupposed for thinking to occur. But, then, I reasoned, if I am not wondering (thinking), do I exist? Descartes said he would not write about anything that has already been dissected or explained by someone else. That would be someone else's thinking and not his. That would be rote memory of someone else's thoughts and not his own.

This is rather like the noted Swiss developmental psychologist, Jean Piaget (1892-1980), who said that if you are not thinking, you have no intelligence; you are simply reciting what others have done or taught you. You would exist through the thoughts of others, but not your own. Thinking, therefore, is like intelligence; if you are not mentally acting on something you really do not exist – like a doll or robot that can only do what others want it to do, with no existence of its own.

> It has been said that Descartes was having a snack at a Parisian sidewalk cafe and afterwards the waiter asked if he would like a dessert. In reply Descartes answered, "I think not." The waiter then asked Descartes, "Does that mean you do not exist?"

Thinking is active involvement in finding solutions that no one has thought about before. That is when we can say, "I exist" in my own right and not merely through the thoughts of others.

All of this is not to suggest that we should not concern ourselves with what has gone on before. Of course, in our youth we should devour the great books of the world, travel and mix with all kinds of people high and low, experience everything possible in many situations, and constantly reflect on every experience to profit from each one. All of this is to begin to exist – to think, to be "I am". Only then can one say, "I have learned what science says, what math says, what religion says, and much more. I can find relationships through it all and I can think." Then one can say, **I think, therefore, I am.**

And if I do not think – use my intelligence – I am not.

Kindness Is The Beginning Of Cruelty.

Frank Herbert (1920-1986)

WE ALL know about "Do unto others...." Some may even try to live by this because it is not only the right thing to do, but it is also a kind thing to do. But then here comes an aphorism that says kindness can actually be cruel. How can that be? What can be wrong with being kind? Much less cruel? How could Frank Herbert, a science writer and scholar, be right?

People who study words such as "kindness" and "cruel" – semanticists - tell us that "kindness" and "cruelty" are opposites, just as physics has shown that magnets have opposite forces. If the word "kindness" means an act of helpfulness, good will, and generosity and "cruel" implies an act of indifference or even a willingness to cause distress or unhappiness, then how can one lead to the other?

Consider the Biblical injunction: "The Lord giveth and the Lord taketh away," or even closer to home, "The government giveth and the government taketh away." Some of the native Americans in Canada give us an example of how an effort to be kind has led to unhappiness or even cruelty. They have noted that even though they were given territories, schools, and many other benefits the government "Took our pride, our dignity, and the things that make you a living soul." A kindness turned cruel.

The welfare system in the United States has been cited and criticized for giving monetary handouts where it is needed instead of providing programs to help people become self-sufficient. The generous act of kindness may have been turned into something unsatisfactory or cruel by taking away the pleasure of self-sufficiency because of learning to rely on gifts from others. The effort to help and be kind may have turned in many instances to be harmful or even cruel.

Kindness has many attributes: sympathy, gentleness, tenderheartedness, and even altruism. What needs to be done is to turn the various ways of using these attributes so that they are understood as kindness and not just acts that provide a feel-good experience or of being kind for the purpose of getting something in return. Obviously, we do not want to be sympathetic or even altruistic simply because of the temporary benefits of being kind.

Kindness can be mistaken even when no selfish motives have been intended. We may hear, "You hurt my feelings. Why did you do that?" This points out that the way kindness is expressed may be as important as the kind act itself because of the danger of perceiving it differently than intended. Cruelty may not have been the motive but it may have been perceived to be.

Genuine kindness begets kindness, but it can also beget dissatisfaction, anger and even cruelty if we do not use it thoughtfully and sincerely.

A Thing Of Beauty
Is A Joy Forever.

John Keats (1795-1821)

WHEN SOMEONE says, "I like this picture," that is not what John Keats is talking about when he said, **A thing of beauty is a joy forever.** He is not talking about "sofa art." Keats is talking about beauty that elicits great joy and pleasure and happiness. For him, true beauty makes an immense difference in our lives and imparts more than temporary sensual pleasures.

The beauty Keats describes is that beauty which touches our inner being. Some refer to it as "inner beauty." Helen Keller expressed a similar idea when she said, "The most beautiful things in the world cannot be seen or even touched, they must be felt with the heart." The Russian mathematician, Ivan Panin, said it a little differently: "For every truth there is an ear somewhere to hear it. For every love there is a heart somewhere to receive it."

Keats is not talking about the kind of beauty that might be called visceral beauty, that is, beauty which appeals to the senses and feelings rather than to conscious reasoning. The kind of beauty that appeals more to the senses rather than reasoning may be referred to as a beauty of first impressions. For example, some might say, 'She is a beautiful woman," but Keats would probably say that a beautiful woman is that woman who has a heart of love and virtue and whose inner beauty is immortal. Keats is talking about that kind of beauty that calls for an intellectual reaction, rather than first impressions.

Some might say that beauty is physical and sensual and that beauty is in the eye of the beholder. Keats is talking about that kind of beauty which calls for a thoughtful and contemplative reaction and can only be seen with the heart.

Insist On Yourself;
Never Imitate.

Ralph Waldo Emerson (1803-1882)

I T IS difficult to read this aphorism and not think of Benjamin Franklin because of his emphasis on the business of living by being frugal and relying on your own hard work. But it seems to me that Ralph Waldo Emerson takes us a bit deeper into this business of living. While agreeing with Franklin on the significance of industry and thriftiness, Emerson goes a step further by relying on ourselves and stressing the added importance of originality; that is, developing our own individual uniqueness and not falling in lock-step with commonly accepted ideas...not being a carbon copy of some else's ideas.

Self-reliance is Emerson's theme. We must not imitate others nor strive to be like those who have gone before us. People do not become great by looking for examples to follow. The unique person, the great person, is the example. Emerson has said in many ways that greatness is a by-product of uniqueness.

Conformity to societal opinion is the antithesis of self-reliance because, for Emerson, being one of many in a like-minded group is not being unique. Being unique is being ourselves, and not being a duplicate of someone else's thinking or actions. Emerson has put it this way: *"Whoso would be a man must be a nonconformist. A foolish consistency is the hobgoblin of little minds. To be great is to be misunderstood."*

Being a nonconformist can set us apart from the group. Try this: Have you ever been in a group of kindred spirits or like-minded people and they all have read the same books, have seen the same movies and TV shows, subscribe to the same journals and magazines, and laugh at the same jokes — they are like-minded. And then you say something contrary to their views. The group may become quiet or you may even have to leave. Emerson would advise not to conform to such " group-think groups" but be self-reliant even if it is uncomfortable, because, for him, true originality and self-reliance come from *"turmoil and the constant boiling of new insights and ideas."*

To *"insist on yourself,"* therefore, means to persist with yourself even when your church group, your political party, or your bridge club put up resistance. Being a member of like-minded groups tends to lead to conformity and to lose your own self-reliance because to know your church group, your political party, or your professional group is to be able to anticipate your thinking.

So, how can we become great? Not by copying someone else, nor even by being taught, but by being persistently and intellectually true to ourselves. After all. who taught Shakespeare or Franklin or Michelangelo?

Live in the noble principles of your being and rely on them without the dependence on others' opinions.

That which you can do best none can teach you.

Ruling A Large Kingdom Is Like Cooking A Small Fish; The Less Handling The Better.

Tzu Lao

THIS APHORISM is attributed to Lao Tzu, a revered Chinese philosopher and though his exact dates are unknown, it is known that he was a contemporary of Confucius (551-479 BC).

The original wording was: *"Ruling a large kingdom is like cooking a small fish."* Later someone added: *"the less handling the better,"* and that made it a little clearer. Good cooks know that in cooking a fish, too much handling or prodding tends to tear apart the fish. In cooking a fish let it cook itself; turn it a couple times and it will cook very well without any more help.

Similarly, Leo Tzu pointed out, leaders who prod into minutiae too much tend to stir up problems instead of giving guidance and time to let situations work out by themselves. Leaders who direct too much limit their own effectiveness and alienate many people along the way. Attention is constantly divided into too many directions. People soon look to the leader to solve all problems, and we all know that is impossible.

In this regard, Leo Tzu further said, *"A leader is best when people barely know he exists, when his work is done, his aim fulfilled, they will say: 'we did it ourselves'."* The leader is not a non-action person but one who wisely does as little as possible.

Leo Tzu worded it this way:

Be the chief but never the Lord.

He is probably most famous for:

Give a man a fish and you feed him for a day; teach him how to fish and you feed him for a lifetime.

In contemporary thought this could be "less is more." And applied to art, it has been said, "The best sculptors do the least cutting."

Trust In God, But
Tie Your Camel.

THIS SOUNDS like it came out of the Middle East, and
that it did – from Saudi Arabia, but more exactly from
the Prophet Mohammad (570-632 CE), only he used the
word Allah.

This aphorism speaks to the basic fact that no matter
what the belief or religion, some things remain constant. In
this case: untied camels or horses or whatever tend to wander
off, or even stolen. Innocence or blind faith may in fact be
a protection in some situations in life but as a matter of
common sense certain measures must be taken. No amount
of belief will change the reality of living in this world.

The message is self-evident and commendable. God (Allah) gives food, clothing, and shelter, but in the event that nothing is given, it is God's (Allah's) will and we cannot complain. So Mohammad used camels as a metaphor to warn people not to be careless with what they have because losing a camel could actually be losing a livelihood.

The message is: *"God helps those who help themselves."* And in a Russian writing we read: *"Pray to God but keep rowing to shore."* A similar message is related in this Jewish fable:

A great flood came over all the land and water began covering the houses. People were warned to leave for higher ground and they did, except Moishe. He stayed in his room and someone swam past the window and called out to him to join them. But Moishe said, "No. I have no need to leave, God will save me."

As the water rose Moishe had to go upstairs. Then someone rowed past the window and shouted to Moishe, "Come, I have space in my boat." But Moishe said, "No, I have no need to leave, God will save me."

The water kept rising and Moishe climbed out onto his roof. As he was on the verge of drowning, a rescue helicopter came past and shouted down to him to climb up the ladder. But Moishe shouted back, "No, I have no need to leave. God will save me"

The flood kept rising and Moishe drowned. He had been a good Jew so he went to heaven.

When he got there, he met with God and said to God,, "Look here, I had so much faith in you, what happened?" God's reply was, "Moishe, what more do you want me to do? I sent people to encourage you. I sent a boat and even a helicopter."

It's Déjà Vu All Over Again.

"Yogi" Lawrence Peter Berra (1925)

"YOGI" IS noted as the greatest catcher in baseball history. He quit school after the eighth grade and later became famous for his malapropisms, that is, his misuse of words, for example:

"I really didn't say everything I said."

"It ain't over 'til it's over."

When Berra was asked. "What time is it", his answer was, "You mean now?" This may seem to be a rather flippant answer, but it could have a breath of depth to it by reminding us that there is no time like the present. Down deep he may not have been as shallow as he may have appeared to be. Some say he made sense in a wacky way. That is what aphorisms do; the more you think about them the more sense they make.

Déjà vu is not very difficult to define. It means somehow having the memory or feeling of familiarity about something even though it is unfamiliar. By having this feeling of reliving something can be accompanied with a feeling of eeriness or oddness and can be very disconcerting by not understanding this feeling. It is like standing on a hill in Germany overlooking the Rhine River for the first time and saying to yourself, "I feel like I have been here before."

Science has tried to describe the déjà vu sensation. It points out that nearly everyone has a déjà vu experience at least once in their lives. It is also known that it is more common in people under age 25. The most common characteristic of the déjà vu sensation is that it nearly always involves very ordinary events, as opposed to life-shattering events.

Some scientists have tried to describe déjà vu in several ways by using such terms as "precognition" and "recollection", juxtaposing it with short term memory and long term memory. Others have described the phenomenon as events having been stored in the memory before the conscious part of the brain was developed enough to receive and process information.

Others have said that déjà vu is more likely to be associated with an improper electrical discharge in the brain, as in epilepsy. Considerable research has also been done to discover how déjà vu may be related to hypnosis.

But back to "Yogi" Berra. When he said, "I never said most of the things I said," is he speaking for most of us as we think many of our past statements?

"Yogi" was a talker behind the plate. He used to talk to the opposing batters to distract them. Hank Aaron tells the story about the 1968 World Series, with "Yogi" behind the plate. "Yogi" kept telling Aaron to "hit with the label up on the bat." Finally, Aaron turned and said, "Yogi", I came up here to hit, not to read."

A Few More of "Yogi's" Malapropisms

"Baseball is mainly 90 percent mental
and the other half is physical."

"Always go to other people's funeral
otherwise they won't come to yours."

"I always knew that record would
stand until it was broken."

"It gets late early out there."

"Nobody goes there anymore. It's too crowded."

"We have deep depth."

"We made too many wrong mistakes."

One Cannot Step Twice
In The Same River.

Heraclitus (c. 525-c. 475 BCE)

THE FULL aphorism is:

One cannot step twice into the same river, for other waters are ever flowing on to you.

The early thinkers argued about the one thing that formed the basis of all human experience. The final answer was: Change is inevitable. One philosopher said all things were water; another thought air was the basic ingredient; another said that the world was an "everlasting fire." But the common thought was that all these things change from time to time but in the end they are still the same element – constant. Everything is constant even though change in inevitable. The water may have flowed on but it is still a river. Everything that is a basic element of life is complete in itself. Even though the element may contain various attributes, for example, an opposite, cold and hot, the element is complete in its self and so the element is constant. The condition may be hot or it may be cold but it is still the same element.

Some say that even though the basic elements remain the same, the refusal to accept this understanding is the basis of all unhappiness – the refusal to accept how things in life work: death and life, happiness and sadness. Where one thing exists in life the opposite is part of it and one follows the other.

The understanding of this constancy in nature forms the basis for successful living and the virtuous life. The relentless pursuit of one part of nature's elements – wealth, fame, stature – only makes one a psychological slave to the endless activity of ambition and desire and ignoring the completeness of life. Other aphorisms similar to Heraclitus's are:

> **Nothing endures but change.**

> **No man ever steps in the same river twice, for it is not the same river and he's not the same man.**

> **The road up and the road down is one and the same.**

To Own Nothing Is The Beginning Of Happiness.

Epicurus (341-270 BCE)

I<small>S IT</small> true that the possession of things brings personal happiness? Or is it true that owning nothing brings happiness? Or is happiness somewhere between these two extremes?

First, it is difficult to define happiness as a thing. Happiness is a feeling. It is the pleasurable sensation of contentment, or an awareness of pleasure, as in, "I was very happy when I met you." When we are happy we have the feeling of joy or bright spirits, and we are also happy when we are lucky about something. Or philosophers might say that happiness is the feeling of being virtuous or worthy of merit. Or we might say, "A positive attitude is the beginning of happiness."

Second, happiness is being gracious, or not being rude. But an obsession with graciousness is very inconsistent with virtuousness. In fact, an obsession with anything counters feelings of joy and contentment and does not lead to a virtuous life. It is that obsession with things that blinds people to what really matters on the road to happiness. The constant wanting and needing the latest fads sidetracks people in their quest for value and only leads to the next sensation. There is no end in that search for things like 3'D television, whiter teeth, convertibles, a flat stomach, smoother skin, latest styles, or even breath fresheners.

Doing without things may not be the road to happiness, but being the consummate consumer is not either. The trick is to know when enough is enough. It has been said that nothing is sufficient for the man to whom the sufficient is too little. Gluttony does just the opposite – eating too many cheese burgers, running up a huge credit card debt, burning the candle at both ends, This idea of sufficiency is the answer to feelings of happiness. Epicurus has said it many different ways:

> **Nothing is sufficient for people to whom the sufficiency is too little.**

> **Self-sufficiency is the greatest of all wealth.**

> **He, who is not satisfied with little, is satisfied with nothing.**

A person is made unhappy by
    endless or vain desire.

It is better to have an overflowing table
    than have no peace of mind.

Know Thyself.

Ancient Wisdom Writer

I F THERE is one thing in this world I know nothing about it is this. I do not know what **Know thyself** means. And I do not know who said it first. I only know that it is very old. Supposedly, it was written centuries before Biblical times, even before the early Greek philosophers and it keeps popping up in today's high-tech world. It is said that if there were a book written about this topic it would be entitled *"The Wisdom of the Ages."*

Very simply put, **Know thyself** means to examine and analyze ourselves and to do it thoroughly. It is impossible to know and understand the minds of others very well if we have not looked very carefully at our own. **Know thyself** does not mean to condemn nor condone the thinking or the actions of others.

Know thyself tells us to try to understand ourselves, to know our own highlights and lowlifes, to realize our own true and hidden motives, and to discover an honorable and honest way of life. It is to seek new truths in our own minds without relying on others. Benjamin Franklin similarly pronounced that we should observe all people but analyze our own thinking the most. This means the observing and analyzing of others and ourselves in the middle of the milieu of today's world. Another writer has suggested that the way to **Know Thyself** is to write an autobiography describing not only the events in our lives but also describing our likes and dislikes of those events.

Knowing yourself is to live wisely and not be "economical with the truth" about others or ourselves. The key here is self-inquiry, paying no attention to the opinions of others in our lives, both far and near.

Knowing thyself is the only way to arrive at the true answer to, "Who am I?"

Avoid Outshining
Your Superiors.

Balthasar Gracian (1601-1658)

MAKE YOUR superiors feel comfortable even if they are not as brilliant as they think they are. It will help you attain power, and you will be more comfortable, too. This aphorism, therefore, is not about how to be the boss, but how to become the boss.

Something there is about that word *superiority*. One writer stated, "All superiority is odious." Or this may be said another way: "All victories breed hatred" and "Pre-eminence is always hated." A prince wants to be looked up to so that his princely qualities and decisions can be respected. Royalty, bosses, and masters generally want to feel secure in their positions and superior to those around them in wit, charm, and intelligence. They will allow someone to help them, but not surpass them.

You may actually be superior in a number of ways but displaying your talents may accomplish the opposite. In childhood we learned the little song, *"This little light of mine, I'm going to let it shine"* but in adulthood we know that showing off yourself to the boss and the over-display of your talents may have unintended consequences. Resentment, dislike, and envy may arise. That is not to say that we go through life worrying about the feelings of others, but when it comes to those in positions of power or people whom we really want to impress, a different approach must be taken. The worst mistake of all is to outshine the boss or anyone we want to influence – whether it is in public life or in private life.

The trick is to influence those in power in subtle ways. For example, when giving advice to those in superior positions make your advice appear so that as something they have only forgotten rather than as something they do not know or could think of themselves. Or, being assigned a difficult task, take it, do it, and report it as if it were easy. The lesson here is to live a good and successful life; however, if you cannot prevent yourself from showing your intellect or your charm, avoid monstrous displays of it, at least in the presence of those you wish to influence.

The Limits Of My Language Mean The Limits Of My World.

Ludwig Wittgenstein (1889-1950)

WHAT THE aphorism means is this: If we cannot think of it we cannot describe it, and if we cannot think it then it cannot be – at least in our world. For something to exist in our world (in actuality or in our imagination) we must be able to think it. If it does not exist in our world, we cannot think it and therefore we have not the language to describe it. Therefore, our language is limited because the limit of our world is limited by our thoughts.

It was Plato and the philosophy of idealism that insist that if mankind cannot think of it, it doesn't exist, and it was my mother who taught me that if mankind can think it, it does exist, either in actuality or in imagination;.

Have you ever said, "I know what I mean. I just can't put in words"? That means the reality of it clearly does not exist and therefore the language is limited by our ability to know it.

Consider this example: Have you ever heard a selection of music that you dearly love and you would like to describe it so that others could enjoy it also. You can't. Our limited language prevents our ability to describe what it actually is, and we ourselves probably do not know exactly what it sounds like and why we love it so much. We cannot describe it because we really do not know. In this case, our world is limited and consequently so is our language. Our language is limited by the limits of our knowledge.

Some might put it this way: If it is not thinkable by us, it could never register in our minds. To confuse the issue even more, another area of thought says that there are things in existence that are beyond our human ability to imagine, or conceive.

If all of this makes your head swim, we need to ask, "Are there some things that are unknowable?" That is what aphorisms do. Aphorisms make us think beyond what is given.

Wittgenstein was an Austrian writer, thinker, and a philosopher. Some other aphorisms by him are:

What can be shown cannot be said.

If a lion could talk we could not understand him.

The meaning of words is derived
   from their public use.

Someone who knows too much
   finds it difficult to lie.

Learn to be a loser.

The world is the totality of facts, not of things.

For a truly religious man, nothing is tragic.

The Truth Is Rarely Pure And Never Simple.

Oscar Wilde (1854-1900)

TRUTH IS complete and can stand alone without supportive statement or explanation or even without the approval of some authoritative figure or leader, as in, "Just because he said it doesn't make it so." Truth is without condition and is absolute regardless of who said it or wrote it. For example: "Thieves steal" is an absolute truth and stands by itself.

But for Oscar Wilde in Victorian England, he found truth to be different. Truth tended to be found by examining classical texts and personal lifestyle. He was well read in many disciplines but in his pursuit of his interest of art he began to believe truth and art are both "in the eye of the beholder."

For Wilde, the study of religious theology and liturgy were interesting but because of his understanding of truth he refused to believe any formal creed. It was a creed – not a truth.

In later life, at the age of 46, because of his individualism and his "ungentleman-like" behavior, he was arrested and imprisoned for two years. Thoughts he believed to be truths turned out to be used against him and convicted him. Some of those thoughts are:

> A gentleman is one who never hurts
> anyone's feelings unintentionally.

> A little sincerity is a dangerous thing, and
> a great deal of it is absolutely fatal.

> A true friend stabs you in the front.

> A thing is not necessarily true
> because a man dies for it.

Love Decreases When It Ceases To Increase.

Francois-Rene Chateaubriand (1768-1848)

CHATEAUBRIAND WAS a writer, politician, diplomat, historian, and French philosopher, but he is also known as the creator of the Chateaubriand steak (the thick beef fillet cut from the center of the tenderloin). He was a diplomat under Napoleon, but is also considered the father of French Romanticism.

He wanted us to understand that when you are not falling in love you are gradually falling out of love. He insists that it is the temporal love that initially binds but it is the constant and lasting *loving* and the seeking ways to express that love that will make great love. It is the present tense and enduring word, *loving,* that causes love to increase. In the passive tense, *loved,* sentiments become diminished instead of giving great sentiments time to mature into greatness.

> It is the duration of the loving
> sentiments that allows great love.

Interestingly enough, it was the 19th century German philosopher and poet, Fredrich Nietzche (1844-1900), who wrote something similar but in a different context. In speaking about people who have been great he said:

> It is not the strength, but the duration of
> great sentiments that makes great men.

Pleasure Is The Only Good.

Epicurus (341-270 BCE)

THIS IS hedonistic theory, but hedonism words put it this way: "Pleasure is the only intrinsic good…" A first reading of this sounds like our lives should be guided in the pursuit of self-indulgence and happiness. In modern words we should "east, drink, and be merry for tomorrow we shall die," but that is not what the ancient Greek philosopher had in mind.

Epicurus believed that we should lead a life of pleasure but our goal of seeking pleasure should be tempered by morality, serenity, and cultural development. **Pleasure is the only good** holds that pleasure presupposes the absence of pain, particularly when that is caused by extreme desires for wealth, fame, power, or even the pain caused by the fear of death.

To some this aphorism sounds like our 21st century life of rap music, alcohol, and drugs. Hardly. Pleasure is derived by non-participation in the extremes of life and living quietly in the comfort of friends.

Epicurus did not believe in a god and therefore he felt there should be no pain associated with the anticipation of death because there would be no judgment that follows death.

Pleasure is the only good should not lead us to the shameless pursuit of base pleasures of sex, drugs, or one long Bacchanalia. Pleasure is the absence of any kind of pain and discomfort and allows gratification and satisfaction of life.

We Are What We Think.

Gautama Buddha (c568 to 483 BCE – c468 to 483 BCE)

BUDDHA EXPLAINED it this way: "*All that we are is a result of what we have thought. If a man speaks or acts with an evil thought, pain follows him. If a man speaks or acts with pure thoughts, happiness follows him, like a shadow that never leaves him.*"

If Buddha's statement is to be believed, it only follows, doesn't it, that what we think makes a great difference in our lives. Buddha is not talking about our genetic inheritance, or our body type, or our physical being. What he is talking about is how our thinking affects our overall selves. (Not whether you will have red hair and blue eyes.) He explains how our thoughts control our thinking. And how our thoughts can lead to pain, anguish, joy, happiness or even sorrow.

Our real being, our selves, is nothing more than our thoughts. Nothing is real but our thoughts. What we are thinking about, or not thinking about, controls how we act and whatever we do. We are nothing more than our thoughts. Our real self is our thinking and, for Buddha, nothing is real or exists but the self. Therefore, **we are what we think.**

This aphorism is akin to the idea that if a thought never comes into our minds we cannot develop new ideas. And an extension of this leads to this: our thoughts lead to action and our repeated actions lead to habits, and our habits lead to **we are what we think.** Prophet Ezra Taft Benson (1899-1994) said it a little bit differently: *"Thoughts lead to acts, acts lead to habits, habits lead to character, and character will determine our eternal destiny."*

Learn By Doing.

John Dewey (1859-1952)

THE WHOLE process of learning by doing formed the revolutionary thinking in many schools, where education was traditionally something to be passed on from teacher to pupil. With the belief in *learning by doing*, Dewey stressed that real education is growth, therefore:

> Education is not preparation for
> life; education is life itself.

Real education cannot be learned in a vacuum and can best be understood through social interaction. We are not ready-made individuals but we become our true selves by the actions we choose and experience. That is education: learning to deal with consequences of our actions.

What Dewey meant was this: He stressed that things gain meaning by being used in a shared social experience. Shared experience allows the learning to be enlarged and changed as one learns to see from another point of view and the experiences of others. Personal experience and shared experience lead to thoughtful experience when explaining and listening to others.

> **One must learn by doing things. Though you think you know it, you have no certainty until you try it.**

Education would be better to have fewer isolated facts and information in its teaching but it should deal with situations in which facts and information are demanded. Gone should be days when in the elementary school the three R's are mechanically presented in favor of democratic ideal of shared intellectual experiences.

According to Dewey, the goal of education should be *to produce thinkers in a shared experience.* Contrary to this, children tend not to become thinkers as they sit through many hours listening to presentations of facts and information. Children grow in knowledge in dealing with new experiences.

John Dewey was the American philosopher, psychologist, and educational reformer who along with G. Stanley Hall, Charles Sanders Pierce, and William James founded the philosophy of *pragmatism.*

Dewey's quotes and aphorisms are many. Here are a few of them:

> Arriving at one goal is the starting
>   point to another.

> Just as a flower which seems beautiful
>   and has color but no perfume, so are
>   the fruitless words of the man who
>   speaks them but does them not.

> Skepticism: the mark and even the
>   pose of the educated man.

> Luck, bad if not good, will always be with us.
>   But it has a way of favoring the intelligent
>   and showing its back to the stupid.

> The good man is the man who, no matter
>   how morally unworthy he has been,
>   is moving to become better.

Damn With Faint Praise.

Author Unknown
Ancient Wisdom Writer

I N THE literary world (even in Wikipedia) **Damning with faint praise** is considered to be an idiom but its hidden meaning can be so powerful, and even devastating, that I put it in the category of a proverb or an aphorism. The deep hidden meaning is there and the terseness and brevity are there and once you have heard it is difficult to forget. For example: *He lauded his son's great achievements and said his daughter was outstanding, too.* And *the Miami Herald* published this: "*The Miami Dolphins showed the power and strength by almost beating the Denver Broncos.*" (the lowest team in the league).

Damning with faint praise can be a very hurtful thing. It generally does not offer or mention praise for meaningful accomplishments, as in, *"In her quiet way she was a good mother,"* Or this press release on the evening news: *"Members of congress* (actually six Democrats and one Republican) *credited Pres. Obama in the ending of Quddafe's regime."*

Damn with faint praise is more than a backhanded compliment. It is praise at its very least or it is praise that is not very important. It is praise that is minimal, as in, *"Her croquettes were fine."* Such a slight compliment can be mortifying to a dedicated French cook.

That kind of faint praise has been with us for years. Back in c. 110 AD, Favorinus believed that this kind of half-hearted praise could have long lasting and pervasive effects, even bordering on abuse. Phineas Fletcher (1582-1650) wrote: *When needs he must, yet faintly then he praises."* And from Alexander Pope (1688-1744): *Damn with faint praise, assert with civil lear, And without sneering, the rest to sneer."*

Damn with faint praise states a compliment or a praise so vaguely that it may not be a praise at all and may offer more hurt than help. It is surely a way to express an unfavorable opinion or even rejection all the while pretending to be kind and ingratiating, as *"At the Presidential reception they offered delicious little egg salad sandwiches."*

In essence, to **Damn with faint praise** is to compliment so feebly that it implies condemnation. You may want to say something was bad or inappropriate but you want to be nice. One of the examples of is from Dave Barry when he was trying to write a positive recommendation: *Mr. Hitler has always kept his uniform very neat".:* Or in another incident someone wrote this letter of recommendation: *"You would be lucky to get this person to work for you."* Even Shakespeare used faint praise when trying to describe a present king: *"He is better than his predecessor."*

Probably, one of the worse faint praises an aspiring young singer wants to hear is, *"You have great potential."*

Damning with faint praise can be fun, but it can be very hurtful.

Aphorisms From The Famous
And
Not So Famous

Aphorisms

APRECLEIUS APULEUS: Familiarity breeds contempt; while rarity wins admiration.

ARISTOTLE: Pleasure in your work puts perfection in the work.

FRANCIS BACON: It is impossible to love and be wise.

ALEXANDER GRAHAM BELL: When one door closes another door opens, but we often look so long and so regretfully upon the closed door that we do not see the ones which open for us.

Napoleon Bonaparte: He who fears being conquered is sure of defeat.

Napoleon Bonaparte: The most dangerous moment comes with victory.

Edmund Burke: The only thing necessary for triumph is for good men to do nothing.

Carol Burnett: Comedy is tragedy plus time.

James. B Cabell: The optimist proclaims we live in the best of all possible worlds, and the pessimist fears this is true.

Al Capone: You can get more with a kind word and a gun than with a kind word alone.

Marcus Porcius Cato: After I'm dead I'd rather people ask why I have no monument than why I have one.

Confucius: Before you embark on a journey of revenge, dig two graves.

Confucius: I hear and I forget. I see and I remember. I do and I understand.

Joseph Cimino: An excuse is the mark of coward.

Lionel E. Deimel: Faith is the enemy of inquiry.

DEMOSTHENES: To remind a man of the good turns you have done him is very much like a reproach.

DESCARTES: In order to seek truth, it is necessary once in a lifetime to doubt all things.

JUSTICE WILLIAM O. DOUGLAS: Restriction of free thought and speech is the most dangerous of all subversion. It is the one un-American act that could most easily defeat us.

ABBA EBAN: His ignorance is encyclopedic.

ALBERT EINSTEIN: If people are good only because they fear punishment, and hope for reward, then we a sorry lot indeed.

ALBERT EINSTEIN: Unthinking respect for authority is the greatest enemy of truth.

ALBERT EINSTEIN: Make everything as simple as possible, but not simpler.

DWIGHT D. EISENHOWER: Freedom has its life in the hearts, the actions, the spirits of men and so it must be daily earned and refreshed – else like a flower cut from its life-giving, it will wither and die.

RALPH WALDO EMERSON: Imitation is suicide.

EDWARD VII: The thing that impresses me the most about America is the way parents obey their children.

ANATOLE FRANCE: If a million people believe a foolish thing, it is still a foolish thing.

BENJAMIN FRANKLIN: Lost time is never found again.

BENJAMIN FRANKLIN: Power grows mightier with each trial.

ROBERT FROST: The world is full of willing people, some willing to work, and the rest willing to let them work.

ARNOLD GLASOW: The fewer the facts the stronger the opinion.

FRANK HERBERT: Absolute power does not corrupt absolutely; absolute power attracts the corruptible.

EDOUARD HERRIOT: Politics is like a race horse. A good jockey must know how to fall with the least possible damage.

HIPPOCRATES: Life is short, art is long, opportunity fleeting, experimenting dangerous, reasoning difficult.

ADOLPH HITLER: What luck for rulers, that men do not think.

OLIVER WENDELL HOLMES: In nature the judgment upon error is death.

COLLIS P. HUNNINGTON: Whatever is not nailed down is mine. What I can pry loose is not nailed down.

MUMIA ABU JAMAL: Many people say it is insane to resist the system, but it is actually insane not to.

JOHN PAUL JONES: I wish to have no connection with any ship that does not sail fast; for I intend to go in harm's way.

JOHN F. KENNEDY: Forgive, but never forget.

ROBERT F. KENNEDY: Only those who dare to fail greatly can ever achieve greatly.

DALAI LAMA: In the practice of tolerance, one's enemy is the best teacher.

JOHN LOCKE: New opinions are always suspected, and usually opposed, without any other reason but because they are not already common.

DOUGLAS MACARTHUR: There is no security on this earth; there is only opportunity.

MACHIAVELLI: Hatred may be engendered by good deeds as well as bad ones.

KARL MARX: Misery motivates, not utopia.

H. L. MENCKEN: An idealist is one who on noticing that a rose smells better than a cabbage concludes that it will also make better soup.

OLIN MILLER: You probably wouldn't worry about what people think of you if you could know how seldom they do.

MICHEL DE MONTAIGNE: There is no conversation more boring than the one where everybody agrees.

PROPHET MOHAMMAD: To overcome evil with good is good; to resist evil by evil is evil.

TOM MORELLO: You have not converted a man because you have silenced him.

MOTTO OF THE NAVY SEALS: The more you sweat in training the less you will bleed in battle.

NIETZSCHE: What does not destroy me makes me stronger.

EDGAR ALLEN POE: It's not what I feared, but what I had not thought to fear.

ARNOLD PALMER: The road to success is always under construction.

PLATO: No evil can happen to a good man, either in life or after death.

JEAN JACQUES ROUSSEAU: People who know little are usually great talkers, while men who know much say little.

PROPERTIUS SEXTUS: Let no man speak ill of the absent.

GEORGE BERNARD SHAW: Assassination is the extreme form of censorship.

SOCRATES: Those who fail to learn from history are doomed to repeat it.

HERBERT SPENCER: Science is organized knowledge.

THALES: A multiple of words is no sign of a wise man.

THOREAU: It is not what you look at but what you see.

JAMES THURBER: All men should strive to learn before they die, what they are running from, and to, and why.

MARK TWAIN (O. HENRY); It ain't what you don't know that gets you into trouble. It's what you know for sure that just ain't so.

MARK TWAIN (O. HENRY): Loyalty to a petrified opinion never yet broke a chain or freed a human soul.

MARK TWAIN (O. HENRY): Let your ideas ascent from low areas of poetry to the highest spheres of calculation and fact.

LAO TZU: To lead people walk behind them.

VIRGIL: Each of us bears his own Hell.

VOLTAIRE: I may disagree with what you say, but I will fight to the death your right to say it.

VOLTAIRE: If God did not exist, it would be necessary to invent him.

FRIEDRICH VAN SCHLEGEL: An aphorism ought to be entirely isolated from the surrounding world like a little work of art and complete in itself like a hedgehog (porcupine).

OSCAR WILDE: A thing is not necessarily true because someone died for it.

Aphoristic Children's Stories:
Aesop's Fables

Insights From Aesop's Fables

(taken from the internet)

As with the Wisdom Writers, the original Fortune Cookies, and the timeless aphorisms from the great thinkers of the ages, wisdom has also come to us through fables (stories) , the most memorable of which are probably the *Aesop's Fables.* We all remember *The Boy Who Cried Wolf* and *The Fox and the Grapes* (from which the idiom, "sour grapes" comes), and many more.

Who Aesop was is not precisely known, nor exactly when he lived; nor do we know for sure where he lived, or whether he was a Greek or from India. Of interest, however, is the fact that he was a slave, a contemporary of Buddha and he lived in ancient Greece between 620 and 560 BCE. Also, neither Buddha nor Aesop wrote down their thoughts or stories, which were later transcribed by writer/historians.

Aesop's insights give us sharp, but gentle, humor along with lessons in life. He wove a story around humble incidents and then added advice on what to do or not to do. Everyone knows his stories are not true *but they tell a truth*. He, of course, made no claim that his stories were true but he did proclaim the truth that is embedded in the story.

The exact number of Aesop Fables is not known, but there are probably hundreds. Here, in the following pages, are a few of them:

The Old Woman and the Wine Jar

The Old Woman found an empty jar which had lately been full of prime old wine and which still retained the fragrant smell of its former contents. She greedily placed it several times to her nose, and drawing it backwards and forwards said, "O most delicious! How nice must the Wine itself have been, when it leaves behind in the very vessel which contained it is so sweet a perfume!

The memory of a good deed lives.

The Nurse and the Wolf

"Be quiet now," said on old Nurse to a child sitting on her lap. "If you make that noise again I will throw you to the Wolf."

Now it chanced that a Wolf was passing close under the window as this was said. So he crouched down by the side of the house and waited. "I am in good luck today, thought he. "It is sure to cry soon, and a daintier morsel I haven't had for many a long day." So he waited. And he waited, till at last the child began to cry, and the Wolf came forward before the window, and looked up to the Nurse, wagging his tail. But all the Nurse did was to shut the window and call for help, and the dogs of the house came rushing out. "Ah," said the Wolf as he galloped away.

Enemies' promises were made to be broken.

The Boys and the Frogs

Some boys, playing near a pond, saw a number of Frogs in the water and began to pelt them with stones. They killed several of them, when one of the Frogs, lifting his head out of the water, cried out: "Pray stop, my boys, what is sport to you, is death to us."

One man's pleasure may be another's pain.

The Vixen and the Lion

A vixen who was taking her babies out for an airing one balmy morning, came cross a Lioness, with her cub in arms. "Why such airs, haughty dame, over one solitary cub?" sneered the Vixen. "Look at my healthy and numerous litter here, and imagine, if you are able, how a proud mother should feel." The Lioness gave her a squelching look, and lifting up her nose, walked away, saying calmly, "Yes, just look at that beautiful collection. What are they? Foxes! I've only one, but remember, that one is a Lion."

Quality is better than quantity.

The Monkeys and Their Mother

The Monkey, it is said, has two young ones at each birth. The Mother fondles one and nurtures it with the greatest affection and care, but hates and neglects the other. It happened once that the young one which was caressed and loved was smothered by the too great affection of the Mother, while the despised one was nurtured and reared in spite of the neglect to which it was exposed.

The best intentions will not always ensure success.

The Wolf and the Kid

A Kid was perched up on the top of a house, and looking down saw a Wolf passing under him. Immediately he began to revile and attack his enemy. "Murderer and thief," he cried, "What do you here near honest folks' houses? How dare you make an appearance where your vile deeds are known?"

"Curse away, my young friend," said the Wolf.

It is easy to be brave from a safe distance.

Hercules and the Waggoner

A Waggoner was once driving a heavy load along a very muddy way. At last he came to a part of the road where the wheels sank half-way into the mire, and the more the horses pulled, the deeper sank the wheels. So the Waggoner threw down his whip, and knelt done and prayed to Hercules the Strong. "O Hercules, help me in this my hour of distress," quoth he. But Hercules appeared to him, and said:

"Tut, man, don't sprawl there. Get up and put your shoulder to the wheel."

The Gods help them that help themselves.

The Frogs and the Well

Two Frogs lived together in a marsh. But one hot summer the marsh dried up, and they left it to look for another place to live in: for frogs like damp places if they can get them. By and by they came to a deep well, and one of them looked down into it, and said to the other, "This looks a nice cool place. Let me jump in and settle here." But the other, who had a wiser head on his shoulders, replied, "Not so fast, my friend. Supposing this well dried up like the marsh, how should we get out again?"

Look before you leap.

The Dove and the Ant

The Ant, going to a river to drink, fell in, and was carried along in the stream. A Dove pitied her condition, and threw into the river a small bough, by means of which the Ant gained the shore. The Ant afterward, seeing a man with a fowling-piece aiming at the Dove, stung him in the foot sharply, and made him miss his aim, and saved the Dove's life.

Little friends may prove great friends.

The Ass and the Purchaser

A man who wanted to buy an Ass went to market and, coming across a likely-looking beast, arranged with the owner that he should be allowed to take him home on trial to see what he was like. When he reached home, he put him into his stable along with the other asses.

The newcomer took a look round, and immediately went and chose a place next to the laziest and greediest beast in the stable. When the master saw this he put a halter on him at once, and led him off and handed him over to his owner again. The latter was a good deal surprised to see him back so soon, and said, "Why do you mean to say you have tested him already?" "I don't want to put him through any more tests," replied the other. "I could see what sort of beast he is from the companion he chose for himself."

A man is known by the company he keeps.